THE CREATION

A POEM BY
JAMES WELDON JOHNSON

PICTURES BY
CARLA GOLEMBE

Little, Brown and Company
Boston   Toronto   London

For my parents, Stan and Thelma Golembe,
with love and appreciation

And thank you, Hawaii, for showing me the birth of the earth

C. G.

First Edition

Poem text is from *God's Trombones,* by James Weldon Johnson. Copyright 1927 by
The Viking Press, Inc. Copyright © renewed Grace Nail Johnson, 1955.
Published by arrangement with Viking Penguin, a division of Penguin Books USA Inc.

Library of Congress Cataloging-in-Publication Data

Johnson, James Weldon, 1871–1938.
    The creation : a poem / by James Weldon Johnson ; pictures by Carla Golembe.
— 1st ed.
    p.   cm.
    Summary: A poem based on the story of creation from the first book of the Bible.
    ISBN 0-316-46744-8
    1. Creation — Juvenile poetry.   2. Children's poetry, American.
    [1. Creation — Poetry.   2. American poetry — Afro-American authors.
    3. Bible stories — O.T.]   I. Golembe, Carla, ill.   II. Title.
    PS3519.02625C73   1993
    811'.52 — dc20   92-24304

10 9 8 7 6 5 4 3 2 1

HR

Published simultaneously in Canada by Little, Brown & Company (Canada) Limited

Printed in the United States of America

Calligraphy by Barbara Bash

The pictures in this book are monotypes, or one-of-a-kind prints. The process is a
combination of painting and printmaking. A painting is made using oil-based inks on a
piece of Plexiglas. Then while the painting is still wet, it is transferred to paper by means
of an etching press. After the print is dry, it is often worked into again with oil pastels,
colored pencils, or gold and silver Japanese tea chest paper.

And God stepped out on space,
And he looked around and said:
I'm lonely —
I'll make me a world.

And far as the eye of God could see
Darkness covered everything,
Blacker than a hundred midnights
Down in a cypress swamp.

Then God smiled,
And the light broke,
And the darkness rolled up on one side,
And the light stood shining on the other,
And God said: That's good!

Then God reached out and took the light in his hands,
And God rolled the light around in his hands
Until he made the sun;
And he set that sun a-blazing in the heavens.
And the light that was left from making the sun
God gathered it up in a shining ball
And flung it against the darkness,
Spangling the night with the moon and stars.
Then down between
The darkness and the light
He hurled the world;
And God said: That's good!

Then God himself stepped down —
And the sun was on his right hand,
And the moon was on his left;
The stars were clustered about his head,
And the earth was under his feet.
And God walked, and where he trod
His footsteps hollowed the valleys out
And bulged the mountains up.

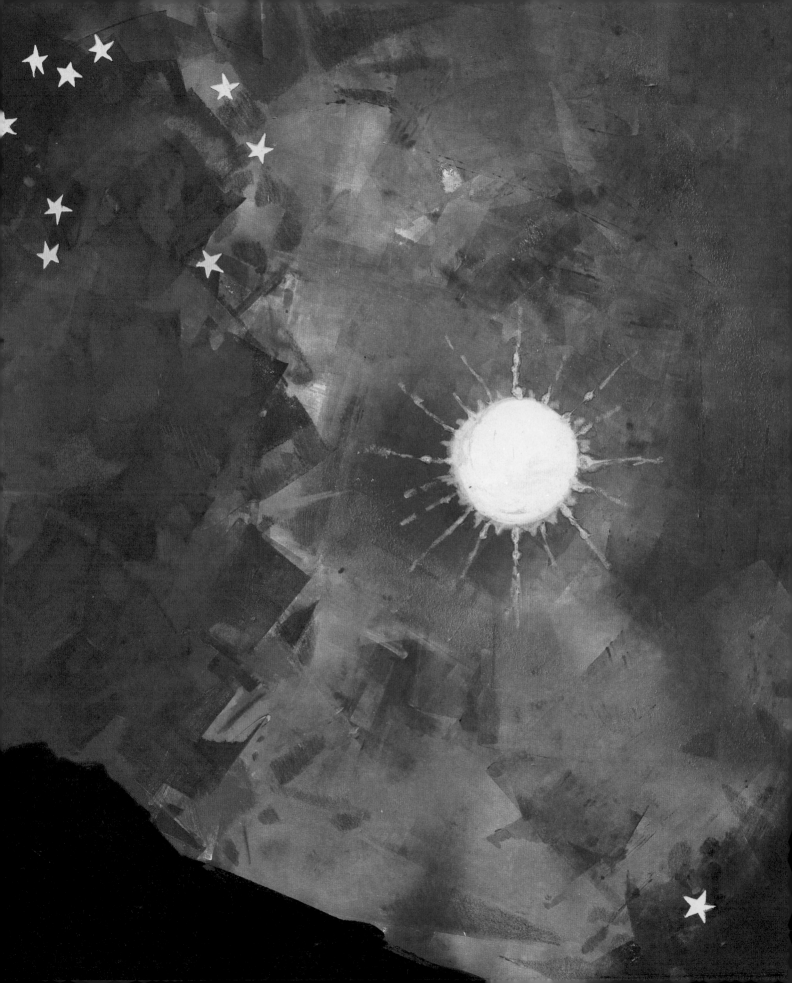

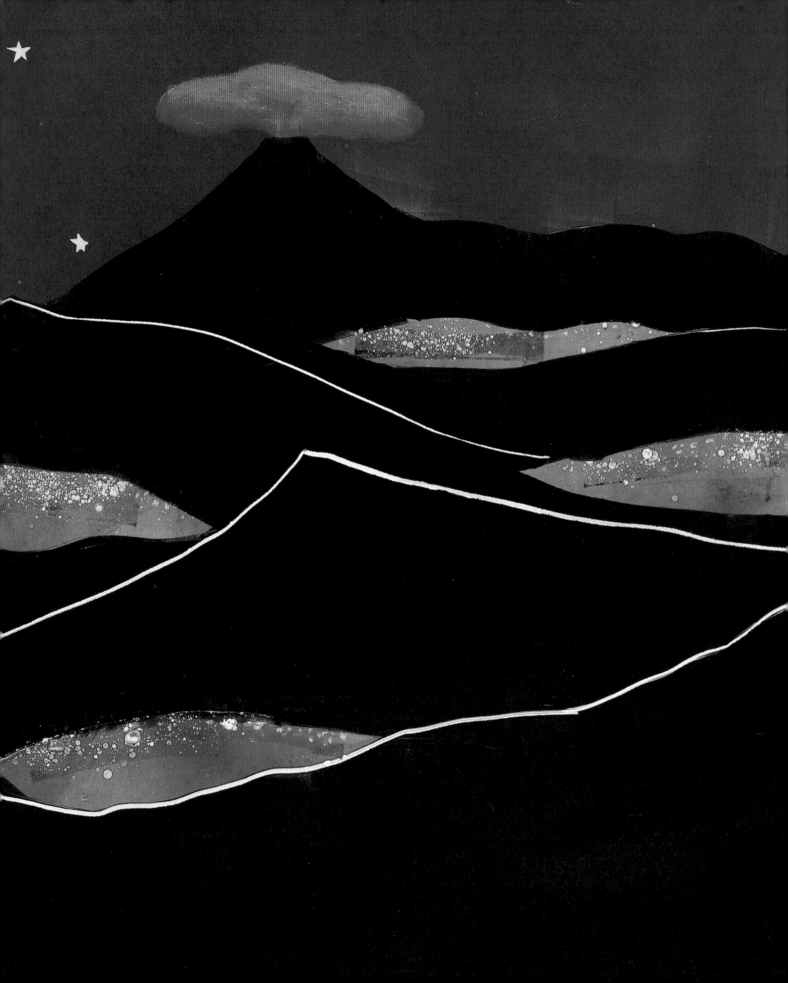

Then he stopped and looked and saw
That the earth was hot and barren.
So God stepped over to the edge of the world
and he spat out the seven seas —

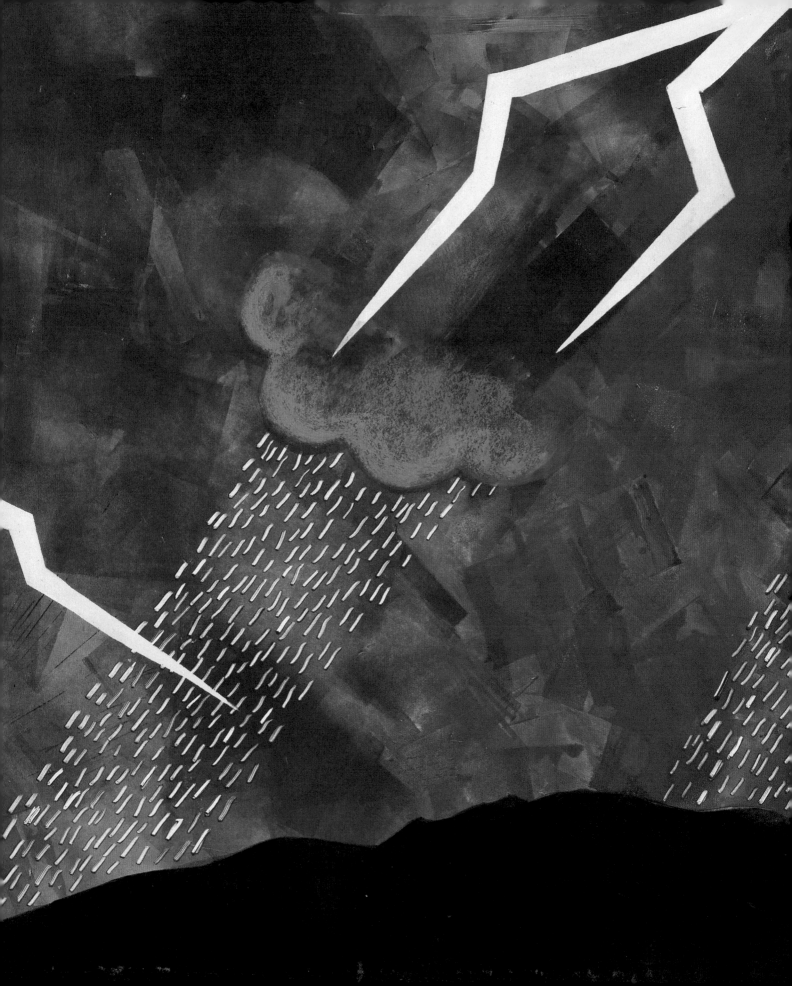

He batted his eyes, and the lightnings flashed —
He clapped his hands, and the thunders rolled —
And the waters above the earth came down,
The cooling waters came down.

Then the green grass sprouted,
And the little red flowers blossomed,
The pine tree pointed his finger to the sky,
And the oak spread out his arms,

The lakes cuddled down in the hollows of the ground,
And the rivers ran down to the sea;
And God smiled again,
And the rainbow appeared,
And curled itself around his shoulder.

Then God raised his arm and he waved his hand
Over the sea and over the land,
And he said: Bring forth! Bring forth!
And quicker than God could drop his hand,
Fishes and fowls
And beasts and birds
Swam the rivers and the seas,

Roamed the forests and the woods,

And split the air with their wings.
And God said: That's good!

Then God walked around,
And God looked around
On all that he had made.
He looked at his sun,
And he looked at his moon,
And he looked at his little stars;
He looked on his world
With all its living things,
And God said: I'm lonely still.

Then God sat down —
On the side of a hill where he could think:
By a deep, wide river he sat down;
With his head in his hands,
God thought and thought,
Till he thought: I'll make me a man!

Up from the bed of the river
God scooped the clay;
And by the bank of the river
He kneeled him down;
And there the great God Almighty
Who lit the sun and fixed it in the sky,
Who flung the stars to the most far corner of the night,
Who rounded the earth in the middle of his hand;
This Great God,
Like a mammy bending over her baby,
Kneeled down in the dust
Toiling over a lump of clay
Till he shaped it in his own image;

Then into it he blew the breath of life,
And man became a living soul.

Amen.

Amen.

James Weldon Johnson wrote this powerful poem in 1919, and it was ultimately published in 1927 in a collection called *God's Trombones: Seven Negro Sermons in Verse.* A respected patriarch of the Harlem Literary Renaissance, Mr. Johnson was first inspired to set down this vivid version of the creation after hearing a dramatic and deeply moving sermon by a black country preacher in Kansas City. Trying to capture and preserve the kind of rich, colorful sermons he had heard as a child, Mr. Johnson also wanted to pay tribute to the old-time black preacher whom he felt had played such a critical role in African-American history. "It was through him," Mr. Johnson wrote in his introduction to *God's Trombones,* "that the people of diverse languages and customs who were brought here from diverse parts of Africa and thrown into slavery were given their first sense of unity and solidarity. He was the first shepherd of this bewildered flock." Like African-American spirituals, these inspirational sermons are a highly imaginative and lasting form of black folk art and its great oral tradition.